EXPLORING
CAREERS

Careers in Architecture and Construction

Barbara Sheen

ReferencePoint Press®

© 2016 ReferencePoint Press, Inc.
Printed in the United States

For more information, contact:
ReferencePoint Press, Inc.
PO Box 27779
San Diego, CA 92198
www.ReferencePointPress.com

LIBRARY OF CONGRESS CATALOGING-IN-PUBLICATION DATA

Sheen, Barbara, author.
  Careers in architecture and construction / By Barbara Sheen.
    pages cm. -- (Exploring careers)
  Includes bibliographical references and index.
  ISBN 978-1-60152-806-3 (hardback) -- ISBN 1-60152-806-X (hardback) 1. Architects--Juvenile literature. 2. Architecture--Vocational guidance--Juvenile literature. 3. Construction industry--Vocational guidance--Juvenile literature. I. Title.
  NA2555.S54   2016
  720.23--dc23
                                                                                            2015026624

Contents

Design, Construct, and Maintain

Professionals in the field of architecture and construction are involved in the design, construction, and maintenance of buildings and other structures. Their work helps society function, and it improves the quality of people's lives. These professionals supply families with homes, businesses with commercial space, sports teams with stadiums, and commuters with highways, among other contributions.

For many who work in architecture and construction, this industry provides personally fulfilling work. As blogger and construction manager Ned Pelger explains on the *Construction Knowledge* blog: "The pride of accomplishment in construction surpasses almost any other industry. We get to be right in the middle of creating and building all sorts of cool stuff, from cathedrals to smart lighting controls. . . . I understand other industries also give a sense of accomplishment . . . but few industries pack the whallop of watching a building rise out of the ground."

A Bright Future

Architecture and construction are among the fastest-growing job sectors in the United States. The Bureau of Labor Statistics (BLS) predicts that between 2012 and 2022, job growth among all professions will grow by about 10 percent. In contrast, job growth in architecture and construction is projected to increase by 21 percent. That translates to about 1.6 million new jobs—the highest among all goods-producing sectors and the third highest among all major industry sectors.

4

Many Choices

Jobs in architecture and construction take many forms. Individuals interested in this sector can choose from a wide variety of career paths. Those who want to pursue careers in design can become architects—professionals who design buildings. Or if they prefer designing structures like bridges and roads, they may opt to be civil engineers. Urban planners, too, are designers. They focus on planning and designing whole communities such as new subdivisions. They are also responsible for joining new communities with existing ones.

Other professionals, known as environmental engineers, design systems to control waste. Through their work, they help make the earth a safer and cleaner place. Landscape architects also help enhance the environment. They plan and design outdoor spaces like parks, golf courses, and scenic roadways. Additional design professionals, known as interior designers, focus on beautifying indoor environments. These professionals design and decorate the interior of buildings. Their work includes selecting lighting fixtures and decorative aspects like window treatments and furniture, as well as coordinating colors and materials.

There are also many opportunities for individuals interested in building. They can become carpenters, construction professionals who work with wood, or ironworkers, who work with steel—often on tall structures at high elevations. Or they can decide to work with bricks and stones and pursue a career as a mason. Artistic people can become tile or marble setters. These professionals set tile and marble in intricate patterns over floors and walls. Other professionals are needed to assemble, install, and repair electrical and plumbing systems; still others install and repair roofs and solar energy systems. Construction professionals also drive heavy construction equipment. All of these workers are supervised by construction managers; they oversee the many components involved in a construction project.

Other career opportunities exist for individuals who do not directly design or build but are nevertheless essential to the construction process. For instance, before work on a structure begins, surveyors take measurements of the building site to establish boundary

Projected Change in Construction Employment, by Occupation, 2012–2022

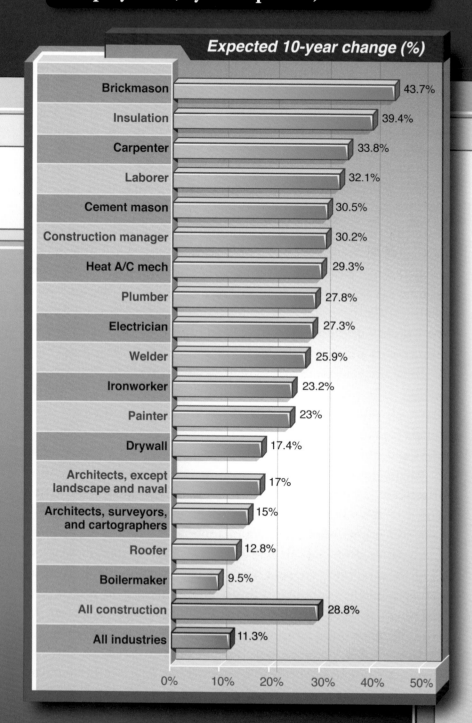

Expected 10-year change (%)

Brickmason	43.7%
Insulation	39.4%
Carpenter	33.8%
Laborer	32.1%
Cement mason	30.5%
Construction manager	30.2%
Heat A/C mech	29.3%
Plumber	27.8%
Electrician	27.3%
Welder	25.9%
Ironworker	23.2%
Painter	23%
Drywall	17.4%
Architects, except landscape and naval	17%
Architects, surveyors, and cartographers	15%
Roofer	12.8%
Boilermaker	9.5%
All construction	28.8%
All industries	11.3%

Source: US Bureau of Labor Statistics, "2012–2022 Employment Projections," 2015. www.bls.gov.

lines. Cost estimators, too, are involved in preconstruction. These professionals calculate the cost of construction projects. Other experts, known as construction inspectors, act like detectives. They examine already-constructed structures to make sure they meet building codes and safety standards. These professionals' work helps keep people safe. As Arizona construction inspector David Swartz explains in an interview on the Job Shadow website: "At times we discover serious safety defects that can hurt or even kill people so theoretically you could say that we help to prevent tragedies and in that way benefit humankind in a major way."

A Place for Everyone

Since architecture and construction is such a broad career field, individuals with differing skills, interests, and education levels can all find a place in this industry. There are positions for active individuals who are mechanically inclined and like to work with their hands, as well as for those who prefer more sedentary work. And, since most work in this sector differs from day to day, individuals who enjoy variation in their work are well suited to a career in architecture and construction. Moreover, many professionals in this sector are self-employed, making this career field a good match for self-motivated individuals who enjoy the challenge and freedom of being their own boss. Conversely, people who prefer the security of working for others can also find work in this sector.

There are many routes a person can take in pursuit of a career in architecture and construction. Some occupations in this sector require a minimum of a four-year college degree. Other positions require that individuals take courses relevant to the career at a community college or trade school. Many jobs in construction, however, do not demand any formal education beyond high school. Instead, they require that candidates do an apprenticeship in their chosen profession. Apprentices are paid professionals who work under the supervision of licensed professionals. Rather than learning in a classroom setting, apprentices learn their trade through hands-on training and experience.

Moreover, even without an advanced degree, many of the jobs in this career field offer lucrative salaries. And architecture and construction professionals are not limited to working in any one geographical area. Opportunities exist for these professionals all over the globe. As British civil engineer Dan Moran says in a 2014 interview on the website Born to Build: "If you are a person who wants to be challenged, meet all types of people and have the chance to work anywhere in the world then the construction sector is for you."

Architect

Architects are artists who plan and design buildings. Their work can include anything from a single room to a multiple building complex. In creating their designs, they take into consideration the look of the building; its function, safety, and cost; and the needs of the client.

Before starting on a design, architects meet with clients to discuss the client's requirements, budget, and objectives for the project. Next, architects research zoning laws, environmental concerns, and fire regulations that may impact the project, since it is essential that the building meet all public safety standards. Once all of this is established, architects begin drawing up plans for the structure. They usually create the first draft by hand but use specialized software to generate the final plans. These are three-dimensional and quite detailed, covering everything from the building's appearance and dimensions to geographic information about the building site and the placement of the structure. Other accompanying diagrams describe the building's electrical, heating and cooling, and plumbing systems, and the

At a Glance:

Architect

Minimum Educational Requirements
Bachelor's degree

Personal Qualities
Artistic
Mathematical

Certification and Licensing
State license

Working Conditions
Indoors, with outdoor visits to job sites

Salary Range
About $44,940 to $121,910

Number of Jobs
As of 2015 about 107,400

Future Job Outlook
Better than average

Architects review their design plans for a new construction project. Whether designing a single room or a multiple building complex, architects must consider looks, function, safety, and cost, as well as the needs and wishes of the client.

location and size of beams, windows, and doors. A project specification report, also prepared by the architect, accompanies the plans. This is a written report, which describes all the specific materials that will be used in the project. For example, the report might include the type, color, and brand of paint to use on exterior steel. In order to compile specification reports, architects spend hours researching different building materials.

While working on a project, architects collaborate with many other professionals. They consult with engineers, urban planners, and landscape architects about different building issues. They may also work with a surveyor and a construction cost estimator. The former measures the boundaries of the construction site, while the latter helps determine the cost of the project. Architects are also responsible for acquiring building permits and helping clients select a construction manager or general contractor who will supervise the actual construction of the building. Once the construction manager is selected, the architect works with him or her in setting up a construction schedule. In some instances the architect may be involved in the selection of subcontractors such as electricians, carpenters, and plumbers. As construction proceeds, architects visit the job site to make sure all the construction professionals involved in the project follow the design, adhere to the schedule, use the specified materials, and meet work-quality standards. Architects also keep in close touch with their clients. They keep clients apprised of the building's progress and deal with any concerns or questions that clients may have. Indeed, a large part of an architect's job involves coordinating information among the various people involved in a particular project. And since most architects work on multiple projects simultaneously, this means that architects interact with many people every day.

Architects sometimes specialize in one phase of the work, such as building design or compiling specification reports. Some specialize in designing sustainable, "green" buildings that feature designs and materials that are energy efficient and do not harm the environment. Others specialize in the design of a particular type of building. For example, British architect Hala Lloyd has been involved in designing more than thirty hospitals and other medical buildings. As she explains in an interview on the Women Working in Construction website: "I have such a particular passion for healthcare design from which I derive such a feeling of accomplishment and personal pride in having contributed towards making a positive difference to a number of people's lives."

How Do You Become an Architect?

Education

Architects are required to have a minimum of a bachelor of architecture degree. Education requirements vary from state to state, but most states require that architects receive their training through a program accredited by the National Architectural Accrediting Board. Accredited bachelor of architecture programs typically take five years to complete. College graduates with a nonarchitecture bachelor's degree can pursue a career as an architect by earning a master of architecture degree.

High school students who are interested in becoming an architect should take college preparatory courses. Classes in art and design are also essential. They help prepare students for the artistic element of designing buildings. And since architects use computer software to prepare designs and reports, computer science classes are valuable, too.

Classes in arithmetic, geometry, and trigonometry are also important. Architects use mathematics almost every day in their work. As architect Evan Troxel explained on the *Life of an Architect* blog in January 2015: "We are constantly adding and subtracting measurements, thicknesses, volumes and areas. We are responsible for budgets. We work with spreadsheets that tally sizes of spaces and everything has to all add up. We do TONS of geometry, and we love it."

High school math classes help prepare candidates for higher-level college mathematics courses, which are part of this major. Other postsecondary classes focus on the skills individuals need to be an architect. Typical course work includes classes in building design, drawing, and building structure. In these classes students practice both freehand drawing and computer-generated drawing and design. Other courses concentrate on construction management, the history of architecture, and the legal aspects of building design, among other subjects.

Certification and Licensing

Architects are required to be licensed. Although licensing requirements differ by state, in general, to become licensed, candidates must have graduated from an accredited architecture program and have three years of practical work experience under the supervision of a licensed architect. They must also pass the Architect Registration Examination, which is a written test that is administered over a four-day period.

Some individuals also choose to get voluntary certification issued by the National Council of Architectural Registration Board. Such certification is prestigious, indicating that an architect has mastery in the field. It may help individuals advance in their career.

Volunteer Work and Internships

Before obtaining a license, graduates of an accredited architecture program must work for at least three years under the supervision of a licensed architect. This is known as an architectural internship. Such positions are full-time paid positions that prepare candidates for licensure. Architectural interns perform many of the same duties as a licensed architect. They design structures and prepare both hand-drawn and computer-assisted plans and drawings. They also research building codes and write specification reports. As blogger and architectural intern Brinn Miracle explains on the *Architangent* blog: "I design architecture. . . . I have not completed my legal obligations to receive my license yet, but the work that I do daily is architecture."

Competition for architectural intern positions is intense. Prospective architects can improve their chances of being hired by doing an unpaid summer internship in an architecture firm while still in college. In such a competitive field, the connections that a summer intern makes, and the on-the-job training and experience he or she receives, helps individuals secure a paid position upon graduation. In addition, some states allow architecture students who complete an internship while they are still in school to count it toward their three-year prelicensure training period.

Skills and Personality

Architects combine the skills of an artist with those of an engineer. In order for the structures they design to be aesthetically pleasing, architects need a good sense of design. They also must have an understanding of space and dimensions. They must be able to visualize spatial relationships and apply geometric principles involving ratios, proportions, and symmetry in their designs. Being able to draw these designs, both freehand and with specialized software, requires that they have strong drawing skills and skill in using drafting software.

In addition, architects should possess good interpersonal and communication skills. They interact with clients and with construction and design professionals. They must be able to get along with and communicate effectively with these individuals. Although architects are not involved in the actual construction of a structure, in order to support and communicate with the various professionals involved in a project and to make informed decisions about the project, architects must be knowledgeable in the basics of structural engineering. This includes understanding wiring, plumbing, heating and cooling systems, and the many other technical elements that go into a structure. Moreover, since architects do not create buildings to please themselves, but rather to satisfy their clients, they must be flexible enough to adapt or change their designs to suit their client's needs. In a July 2014 post on the *Life of an Architect* blog, architect and blogger Bob Borson explains the qualities he looks for when hiring an architect for his firm: "The things I notice above all others is their vocabulary, their ability to speak articulately, and their outside interests. More times than not, I'm not all that focused in on the projects they designed in school. . . . I look at their graphic skills and their ability to frame a story and explain their project."

On the Job

Employers

Most architects are employed by architectural firms. They are also employed by federal, state, and local governments, and by residential and nonresidential construction firms. According to the BLS, approximately one in five architects is self-employed.

Working Conditions

Architects spend most of their time indoors in an office setting, where they meet with clients and create designs. They also visit building sites to review the progress of a project and to make sure the client's objectives are being met. These visits may entail walking on uneven ground through dirt, mud, or dust. Architects wear hard hats during these visits.

Most architects work a standard forty-hour workweek. However, according to the BLS, they may be required to work longer hours to meet deadlines. Self-employed architects set their own hours. Because they must handle both the technical aspects of being an architect and the duties related to running a business, self-employed architects are likely to work as many as fifty hours per week.

Earnings

An architect's salary depends on the individual's education and experience. The BLS reports that as of 2014, salaries for architects ranged from about $44,940 to $121,910, with a mean salary of about $80,490. The BLS reports that mean wages are highest in the following states: California, $92,220; New Jersey, $90,350; Delaware, $89,690; and Massachusetts, $87,880. Individuals employed by the government or by architectural or construction firms usually receive employee benefits that include paid sick and vacation days, health insurance, and retirement benefits. Self-employed architects do not receive these benefits.

Opportunities for Advancement

Upon obtaining a license, architects are usually assigned more complex projects. With greater responsibility comes higher wages. Experienced architects with proven skills may advance to a managerial position in which they supervise other architects. They can become partners in large architecture firms, or they can strike out on their own and establish their own business.

What Is the Future Outlook for Architects?

According to the BLS, between 2012 and 2022 employment for architects is predicted to increase by 17 percent, which is greater than average for all occupations. Demand is expected to be greatest for architects with knowledge of green, or sustainable, design. This is because growing public interest in the environment combined with rising energy costs has increased the demand for sustainable construction.

Find Out More

American Architectural Foundation (AAF)
740 15th St. NW, Suite 225
Washington, DC 20037
phone: (202) 787-1001
e-mail: info@archfoundation.org
website: www.archfoundation.org

The AAF is an organization of architects, urban planners, and other individuals interested in the environmental future of cities. It offers information on careers in architecture and architecture scholarships.

American Institute of Architects (AIA)
1735 New York Ave. NW
Washington, DC 20006-5292
phone: (800) 242-3937
e-mail: infocentral@aia.org
website: www.aia.org/index.htm

The AIA is a professional organization of architects. It provides information about a career as an architect, architectural internships, architectural issues and news, job postings, and scholarships.

American Institute of Architecture Students (AIAS)
1735 New York Ave. NW
Washington DC 20006-5292
phone: (202) 626-7472
e-mail: mailbox@aias.org
website: http://aias.org

The AIAS is an organization composed of architecture students. It provides information about accredited architectural college programs, matches students with professional mentors, and sponsors conferences and networking opportunities.

Association of Collegiate Schools of Architecture (ACSA)
1735 New York Ave. NW
Washington, DC 20006
phone: (202) 785-2324
e-mail: info@acsa-arch.org
website: www.acsa-arch.org

The ACSA is an organization dedicated to improving the quality of architectural education. It provides information about how to prepare for architecture school, lists of accredited architecture programs, tips on selecting a school, and information about the profession.

Carpenter

Carpenters construct, install, and repair buildings and other structures made of wood and other construction materials, such as drywall and insulation. Some of the structures they work on include homes, commercial buildings, bridges, tunnels, and docks. There is a lot of variation in the work they do and in the settings, which makes carpentry a versatile occupation. These professionals may be general carpenters who work on all types of projects, or they may specialize in residential, commercial, or industrial carpentry. Residential specialists build, repair, and remodel homes. Commercial specialists work on commercial buildings such as hotels, hospitals, and stores, whereas industrial carpenters concentrate on the construction of large projects like bridges, tunnels, and power plants.

Carpenters can further specialize in rough or finish carpentry. Rough carpentry specialists are also known as framers. They construct the parts of buildings like wood frames, subfloors, and rafters that are covered up when a construction project is finished. Rough carpenters involved in the construction of tall buildings or bridges build the supports used for cement footings or pillars. They also build

At a Glance:

Carpenter

Minimum Educational Requirements
High school diploma

Personal Qualities
Detail oriented
Physically fit

Certification and Licensing
Voluntary

Working Conditions
Indoors and outdoors

Salary Range
About $25,640 to $74,750

Number of Jobs
As of 2015 about 617,060

Future Job Outlook
Better than average

17

scaffolding for other construction professionals to stand on.

Finish carpentry specialists build and install items like hardwood flooring, doors, and trim. In an interview on the Careers Out There website, California finish carpentry specialist Gary Katz describes the work of a finish carpenter this way: "[He or she] installs doors and windows on the outside walls and then installs jams for doors and sometimes doors and jams on the inside. And then after the doors and jams are in, the baseboard goes in, just the molding along the floor, then the crown molding goes in which is the molding along the ceilings . . . and after the painters are finished, the carpenters . . . install the hardware on the doors and that would be the locks and the knobs and even the hardware in the bathrooms."

Other areas of specialty can be found in carpentry. Some carpenters specialize in making furniture, cabinets, or staircases. Other individuals, known as scenic carpenters, build sets for movies, television programs, and plays.

Whether specialists or generalists, there is a great deal of similarity in what carpenters do. For example, before starting a construction project, carpenters examine blueprints of the structure, which gives them information about the dimensions of the structure and about the materials to be used. With this knowledge in hand, carpenters begin planning how the work will be done. They use tools to measure and mark the wood. Precise measuring is essential. It ensures that the pieces being cut are the proper size so they fit together correctly. Once the pieces are cut, carpenters use a variety of hand and power tools, such as drills and different kinds of saws, to cut and shape the wood, which they nail, screw, staple, or glue together. To guarantee precision, they check their finished work and make any necessary adjustments.

How Do You Become a Carpenter?

Education

No formal education is required for a job as a carpenter. However, most employers prefer they be at least high school graduates. High school shop classes, especially those in woodworking, help give carpentry candidates some of the skills needed in this profession. Some high schools offer vocational-technical training classes in building trades. If such classes are available, students interested in this career should enroll in them. Such classes provide hands-on training in carpentry and other construction professions. Often these classes combine with a work program that gives individuals a chance to gain experience working in their chosen field.

In addition to vocational classes, academic course work also helps people prepare for the profession. Classes in mathematics, in particular, are important. Carpenters use geometry, trigonometry, and arithmetic in their work. For instance, besides being skilled in measuring, in the course of a construction project, a carpenter may have to determine correct wall height, the roof pitch, the curve of an archway, or the rise of stairs. Knowing how to calculate the perimeter, circumference, and area of various geometric figures makes solving these issues easier.

Carpenters can acquire other skills they need for the profession in a number of ways. Many get informal on-the-job training while working as a laborer or a carpenter's helper. Until they become adept at carpentry, these individuals may be charged with simple tasks like carrying lumber, holding materials and tools for other carpenters, cleaning equipment and work areas, or nailing down subflooring. As they become more proficient in carpentry, they are given more responsibility. That is how Randy, a Kentucky carpenter who owns a hardwood flooring business, started out. In a June 2014 article on the Contractor Talk website, he recalls: "Ever since high school, I've been drawn to wood. Took every available woodshop class available, from Jr high, till graduation. In 1984, I took my first job in construction, working for a general contractor, building ground up customs [new custom homes]. Early in this career path, I questioned whether it was the right choice or not, because as the new guy, I got all the jobs no one else wanted to do. But I stuck with it, paid attention & before long, I wasn't the grunt any longer & the job got a lot more rewarding."

Some people opt for more official training in the form of an apprenticeship. Apprentices are individuals who learn a craft through formal classroom training and work experience under the supervision of an experienced professional known as a journeyworker (or what is sometimes still known as a journeyman). Apprenticeships are paid positions, and the training is free. Apprentices are taught valuable carpentry skills while working on construction projects. They also receive training at a vocational or technical school, which covers blueprint reading, carpentry basics, and construction safety practices, among other courses. Carpenter apprenticeships usually last four years. Apprentices are required to complete a minimum of 144 hours of technical training and 2,000 hours of on-the-job training for each year of the program. Individuals who successfully complete an apprenticeship become journeyworkers. Journeyworkers are considered skilled craftspeople that can work independently and supervise others. Apprenticeship programs are offered by many employers, contractor organizations, and local chapters of the United Brotherhood of Carpenters and Joiners of America (UBCJA) labor union. Some apprenticeship programs are sponsored and monitored by the US government.

Some carpentry candidates take still another route. They enroll in a carpenter training program at a technical or vocational school. Such programs offer students classroom training in the use of tools, blueprint reading, building codes, and basic and advanced carpentry skills. Students who successfully complete the program receive certificates of completion, which tell prospective employers that the individual has the skills and ability to work as a carpenter but do not offer journeyworker status. The length of these programs varies depending on the particular school, but most last two years.

Certification and Licensing

Carpenters are not required to have any particular licenses or certificates. However, carpenters can acquire voluntary certifications from the UBCJA in a variety of specialty skills, including scaffolding construction, fall prevention, and working in confined places. Obtaining specialty certificates may help individuals advance in the field.

Volunteer Work and Internships

There are many ways individuals can explore this career. For instance, volunteering for a charitable organization like Habitat for Humanity, which sponsors group building projects that help needy people, is a good way to learn and practice basic carpentry skills. So is volunteering to build sets for school plays and community theater productions.

Joining a student chapter of the National Association of Home Builders (NAHB) or the Associated General Contractors of America is another good way to learn more about a carpentry career. Chapters are located at high schools, vocational and technical schools, and colleges throughout the United States. These organizations sponsor service projects, workshops, field trips, and networking opportunities for student members. For example, in 2015 members of the University of Massachusetts NAHB chapter built and painted special large wooden boxes used in a clothing drive. These organizations also match students with professional mentors and help students find jobs in the construction industry.

Skills and Personality

Carpenters should like building things and working with their hands. They use a variety of tools in their work. In order to avoid injuring themselves or making costly errors when hammering, sawing, or drilling, they should have good hand-eye coordination, manual dexterity, and mechanical skills. Being detail oriented is also essential. Accuracy in measuring lessens waste and construction errors. For example, imprecise measurements can cause gaps between windows and frames that cause leaks. Measuring correctly takes basic math skills, another important ability that carpenters need.

Carpenters who are self-employed also depend on their math skills. They must bid for jobs. A bid tells a prospective client what the job will cost and what will be included in the work. If the bid is too high, the job will probably be given to another person, and if it is too low the carpenter might lose money rather than make a profit. In preparing a bid, carpenters must figure out how much the job will cost to complete and how much he or she must earn to make a profit. This involves having knowledge of prices of materials, labor costs, and competitors' prices.

In addition to these abilities, carpenters should be physically fit. These professionals often have to carry heavy lumber and equipment. Sheets of plywood, for instance, can weigh up to 100 pounds (45 kg). These construction experts spend lots of time standing on their feet and have to reach, climb, crouch, and kneel for extended periods.

On the Job

Employers

According to the BLS, 36 percent of carpenters are self-employed. Carpenters are also employed by residential and nonresidential general and specialty contractors. They work for government agencies, the movie and television industry, and in the shipbuilding, railroad, and aircraft industries.

Working Conditions

Carpenters work both indoors and outdoors in hot and cold weather. Work schedules vary, with most carpenters working full-time. These men and women may have to climb scaffolding and high ladders or work crouched in a low area like a basement or attic. They are exposed to noise, chemical fumes, dust, and dirt on construction sites. However, each site is different, and working conditions change as carpenters finish one job and move to another.

Although construction professionals follow safety procedures, accidents occur. Nicks and cuts to the hands and fingers are the most common type of injury. Other work-related health hazards include falls and back, eye, and repetitive strain injuries. Lung irritation from exposure to dust and chemicals is also common.

Earnings

Carpenters' earnings depend on the geographic location and the individual's background and experience. Experienced and journeymen carpenters typically earn from 20 to 60 percent more than apprentices. The BLS reports that carpenters' salaries range from about $25,640 to $74,750, with an annual mean salary of about $45,590. As of 2014 the BLS reported the mean annual salary for this profession as highest in the following states: Hawaii, $66,880; Alaska, $66,150; New York, $59,460; and Illinois, $56,860. Benefits such as health insurance, paid vacation and sick days, and pension funds depend on the employer. Generally, professionals working under a union contract receive benefits. Self-employed carpenters do not.

Opportunities for Advancement

Experienced carpenters can advance to supervisory positions over-seeing other carpenters. They can also go into business for themselves as independent carpentry contractors or, because they are involved in the entire construction process, as general contractors or construction managers.

What Is the Future Outlook for Carpenters?

Employment opportunities for these professionals are expected to grow at a much faster-than-average rate. According to the BLS, employment for carpenters is estimated to grow by 24 percent between 2012 and 2022. However, it should be noted that jobs in construction often correspond with economic conditions, increasing when the economy is strong and decreasing during economic downturns.

Find Out More

Build Your Future
NCCER/Build Your Future
13614 Progress Blvd.
Alachua, FL 32615
phone: (386) 518-6500
website: http://byf.org

Build Your Future is dedicated to connecting people with careers in construction. It offers information on various construction careers, job postings, accredited training programs, and industry news.

Home Builders Institute (HBI)
1201 Fifteenth St. NW, 6th Floor
Washington, DC 20005
phone: (800) 795-7955
e-mail: postmaster@hbi.org
website: www.hbi.org

The HBI is an organization dedicated to preparing skilled people for jobs in construction. It offers preapprenticeships, apprenticeships, and training programs, as well as information about the industry.

National Association of Home Builders (NAHB)
1201 Fifteenth St. NW
Washington, DC 20005
phone: (800) 368-5242
website: www.nahb.org

The NAHB is a trade association that represents the home building industry. It sponsors student chapters in secondary and postsecondary schools and provides student members with a wide range of information and events involving the construction industry.

United Brotherhood of Carpenters and Joiners of America (UBCJA)
6801 Placid St.
Las Vegas, NV 89119
website: www.carpenters.org

The UBCJA labor union represents more than a half-million professional carpenters. It offers information about and sponsors apprenticeships and training for carpentry specialties.

Civil Engineer

What Does a Civil Engineer Do?

Civil engineers build big structures. They are involved in the design, construction, management, and maintenance of construction projects such as roads, tunnels, bridges, and dams. They also are responsible for public facilities like airports, railways, and ports. And they are the masterminds behind water, energy, and waste systems. Their work shapes the environment and improves the public's quality of life. For instance, to make sure Americans have access to clean drinking water, civil engineers design, construct, and administer reservoirs and other water intake structures, water treatment plants, and the system of pipes that carry water to homes and waste away from homes. They also help bring water to underserved communities throughout the world. In 2011, for example, American civil engineers helped repair a water system in Haiti after a devastating hurricane. Because of their work, many cases of cholera, a disease caused by drinking contaminated water, were prevented. In a January 2013 article on the American Society of Civil Engineers (ASCE) website, Anthony Cioffi, chair of the construction management and civil engineering technology

At a Glance:
Civil Engineer

Minimum Educational Requirements
Bachelor's degree

Personal Qualities
Mathematical
Good problem solver

Certification and Licensing
State license

Working Conditions
Indoors, with outdoor visits to construction sites

Salary Range
About $52,570 to $128,110

Number of Jobs
As of 2015 about 292,000

Future Outlook
Better than average

department of the New York City College of Technology, explains: "This is a perfect example of what we do as a profession—helping people, especially in a crisis situation."

Other civil engineers devise structures that minimize the threat to people's lives due to natural disasters. Civil engineer Aaron White, for instance, led a team that designed an innovative hurricane-proof, retractable roof for Miami's Marlins Park stadium. Not only does the roof withstand 146-mile-per-hour (235 kph) winds, its innovative design is energy efficient.

No matter the project, a civil engineer's primary concerns are the safety, beauty, environmental soundness, and cost effectiveness of their creations. To ensure these concerns are satisfied, these professionals are involved in every aspect of a project, from preconstruction to the maintenance of completed projects. In the preconstruction phase of a project, civil engineers meet with the client to discuss the proposed project and the client's needs and funding. Next they conduct a study to establish the feasibility of the project. An important aspect of the study is analyzing the building site to make sure it will safely support the project. To do this, civil engineers perform tests to identify the type of soil and bedrock at the site as well as any presence of ground-water—all of which may affect the design and the long-term strength of the structure's foundation. They also review survey maps of the site and data concerning government regulations, environmental issues, existing utilities, and construction and labor costs. Then they prepare a written report documenting what they have learned. If the project proves to be viable, they use design software to draw up detailed plans for the structure. They submit the report and the plans to the client and to appropriate government agencies for approval. They may also speak at community forums in response to public concern about the project.

Once construction begins, civil engineers are charged with setting up timetables, work schedules, and budgets; reviewing job progress; and coordinating and supervising construction. Work on large projects can take years. During this time, these professionals spend a lot of time at the construction site, solving problems as they arise and working closely with a construction manager who oversees the day-to-day operations.

Even when a project is complete, these construction experts are still busy. They are tasked with inspecting and evaluating the structure on a predetermined schedule. During these inspections, they perform stress tests on the structure, prepare written reports of their findings, and do repairs and maintenance to the structure as needed.

Civil engineers can work on diverse projects, or they may specialize in a particular area. The most common specialty field is structural engineering. Structural engineers work on buildings and bridges. In an interview on the PBS website, structural specialist Susan Knack talks about this job. "I investigate why buildings leak and deteriorate and design new construction and repairs to deal with these problems. Sometimes I examine the condition of entire buildings . . . and other times I look at smaller issues—like whether or not a window is properly attached and flashed [weatherproofed]. I do some of this work using industrial rope access, or rappelling, to see the building."

Other specialists include transportation engineers, men and women who focus on the construction of highways and transportation systems; and coastal and ocean engineers, professionals who work on projects that operate in or near the ocean. These include projects involving ports, harbors, and offshore structures, among other activities. Other specialists known as water resource engineers focus on water and waste systems, and geotechnical engineers deal with projects involving rocks, soil, and groundwater. For example, geotechnical engineers design embankments for flood control. Environmental engineers are still another specialty group. These men and women work on systems that help protect the environment, such as those that manage the disposal of hazardous waste and those that reduce the emission of pollutants into the air.

How Do You Become a Civil Engineer?

Education

Civil engineers are required to have a minimum of a bachelor of science degree from a college or university accredited by the Accreditation Board for Engineering & Technology (ABET). Many also hold a master's degree. High school students interested in this career should take college preparatory classes. Since civil engineers use algebra, trigonometry, chemistry, and physics on the job, classes in math and science are especially useful. They help prepare students for more-advanced college-level courses that are required for this major. Classes in technical drawing and computer-assisted drafting are also helpful because civil engineers use these skills in their plans and designs.

Required college classes for prospective civil engineers are quite challenging. Students are required to complete courses in calculus, linear algebra, chemistry, and advanced physics, as well as civil engineering courses that cover topics specific to the profession. These include courses like surveying and measuring, engineering materials, and project planning, among other topics. After completing basic civil engineering course work, students can focus their upper-level course work on classes specific to an area of specialization. As an example, classes for individuals interested in structural engineering might include a class on the elements of steel structures. Most classes are combined with lab work, in which students solve the type of problems they will face as civil engineers by experimenting with various materials and designs.

Certification and Licensing

Civil engineers are required to hold a state license. Requirements vary by state. Obtaining a license involves multiple steps. To begin with, candidates must hold a bachelor's degree from an ABET-accredited school and must successfully pass an eight-hour Fundamentals of Engineering Examination. This qualifies the candidate to hold the title of a civil engineering intern or associate engineer. Depending on the state, to be licensed as a professional engineer, individuals must have four years of work experience in the profession and successfully complete another eight-hour exam. A professional engineering license is required to head up a project and to supervise other civil engineers and technicians.

Volunteer Work and Internships

Working on a large construction project as part of a road or construction crew is a good way for individuals to learn about the profession and gain hands-on experience in this field. Individuals can also learn more about this career by joining a civil engineering club. The ASCE sponsors clubs for high school and college students throughout the United States. Members get to participate in hands-on activities, competitions, and service projects. Members of the Tufts University student chapter, for example, designed and constructed a playground for a local elementary school.

Students can gain even more practical experience by participating in a co-op program at a civil engineering firm while attending college. Participants alternate between periods of full-time employment and classroom study. Working in a co-op program provides students with practical experience in civil engineering under the supervision of licensed professionals. In addition to obtaining important work skills, participants develop professional contacts, which can help them gain full-time employment. In fact, many co-op students go on to be hired by the firm for which they worked.

Skills and Personality

Civil engineers should have an aptitude for math and science, since they use these subjects on the job. They should be analytical and possess good problem-solving skills. Creating solutions to problems is a large part of what civil engineers do. They may be charged with figuring out how to update a crumbling bridge, repair an offshore oil rig, or prevent coastal erosion, among other challenges. These professionals must be able to understand how complex systems work and where problems stem from so that they can come up with workable solutions. Creativity is also essential. Civil engineers often have to think "outside the box" to solve difficult problems. They also use creativity in developing new and innovative structures and systems and in making existing systems work more efficiently.

Being detail oriented is another important trait of successful civil engineers. Overlooking a possible design flaw can have dire consequences. Even a tiny error can cause a system or structure to fail. Therefore, these experts must review every detail of a project from preconstruction to completion. And since these professionals work with many different people, write reports, and speak at public hearings, they must be good communicators who are comfortable working with others.

Employers

According to the BLS, about half of all civil engineers are employed by architectural and engineering firms. Others work for local, state, and federal government agencies. Some are self-employed.

Working Conditions

Civil engineers work indoors in offices. They also spend time outdoors at construction sites. Since many firms are involved in global projects, these professionals may have to travel or live abroad while working on a particular project. Most civil engineers work full time. They may be required to work more than a forty-hour workweek in order to ensure deadlines are met.

Earnings

The BLS reports that as of May 2014, salaries for civil engineers range from about $52,570 to $128,110. It reports that the mean annual salary for this profession is about $87,130. Wages are based on an individual's education, licenses, experience, and the geographic location of the firm. Top-paying firms are typically located in large metropolitan areas. With the exception of self-employed individuals, most civil engineers also receive employee benefits. These usually include health insurance, paid sick and vacation days, and retirement benefits.

Opportunities for Advancement

Once civil engineers earn a professional license, they are given more responsibility and compensation. Successful civil engineers with many years of experience can move to managerial positions in which they supervise teams of civil engineers. They can also start their own firm.

What Is the Future Outlook for Civil Engineers?

The future is bright for civil engineers. The BLS predicts that between 2012 and 2022, employment opportunities for this career should grow by about 20 percent. This is double the average for all occupations. As James E. Davis, former executive director of the ASCE, explains in an interview on the Career Cornerstone Center website: "You can't have civilization without having civil engineers. We build the quality of life, we maintain the quality of life. And as long as people have a demand for higher and higher quality of life there'll be a demand for civil engineers."

Find Out More

American Society for Engineering Education (ASEE)
1818 N St. NW, Suite 600
Washington, DC 20036-2479
phone: (202) 331-3500
website: www.asee.org

The ASEE is an organization that promotes engineering education. It offers a variety of publications dealing with engineering, videos, conferences, and information about scholarships for students.

American Society of Civil Engineers
1801 Alexander Bell Dr.
Reston, VA 20191-4400
phone: (800) 548-2723
website: www.asce.org

This organization represents civil engineers. It sponsors student clubs and provides information about civil engineering and about licenses, scholarships, and academic training for the career.

Institute of Civil Engineers (ICE)
1 Great George St.
Westminster, London, SW1P 3AA
website: www.ice.org.uk

The ICE is an international association that promotes civil engineering. It offers information about the career and its history.

Science Buddies
website: www.sciencebuddies.org

The website provides information about careers in science. The article on civil engineers offers lots of information about the career, including an interview with a civil engineer and an article on a day in the life of a civil engineer.

Construction Manager

Construction managers are also known as project managers, general contractors, or construction supervisors. These professionals oversee all types of building projects from conception to completion. As experts in building planning, construction, scheduling, and overall project management and control, they play many roles. For instance, at the start of a project, construction managers meet with clients and consult with architects and civil engineers to review blueprints and project plans. Once they understand what the project entails, construction managers obtain building permits and licenses. When construction begins, they make sure every aspect of the work meets building codes. Another of their responsibilities is creating a construction schedule and ensuring deadlines are met. They hire and supervise the many subcontractors, like roofers, carpenters, electricians, and

At a Glance:
Construction Manager

Minimum Educational Requirements
High school diploma

Personal Qualities
Good interpersonal and leadership skills
Good communicator

Certification and Licensing
Voluntary

Working Conditions
Indoors, with outdoor visits to job sites

Salary Range
About $50,990 to $150,250

Number of Jobs
As of 2015 about 485,000

Future Job Outlook
Better than average

plumbers, who work on the structure. They set and enforce a budget for the project and order building materials and tools. In order to make sure costly materials and equipment are not wasted or used improperly, they keep an inventory of all supplies and equipment. As Minnesota construction manager Joanna Slominski explains in a 2015 interview on the ISEEK website: "I manage subcontractors. Together, we coordinate details in the field, manage schedules, coordinate construction activities, procure materials, and get everything ready and organized so that we can install a project based on the overall schedule. Currently, I'm working on a project at the Minnesota Zoo. . . . We're building a new penguin exhibit, a new bird theater, and a new education space for the zoo."

How Do You Become a Construction Manager?

Education

There are many educational paths prospective construction managers can take. At a minimum, these building experts should have a high school diploma. Through years of work experience, individuals without postsecondary training can learn the different aspects of construction science and work their way up to construction management. However, many construction managers have an associate's or a bachelor's degree. In fact, a number of firms prefer construction managers to have both work experience and a degree from a college accredited by the American Council for Construction Education, an organization that promotes and accredits construction education programs.

No matter what educational path a candidate follows, individuals can start preparing for this career in middle and high school by taking industrial arts classes. Woodworking, metal shop, electronics, and computer-assisted drafting classes, in particular, give students the opportunity to learn some of the skills and use the tools that construction managers employ. Business-related classes such as business math and accounting are useful, too. They help prepare future construction supervisors to deal with budgets and schedules. And classes in speech and language arts help students develop communication skills, which these professionals use in dealing with clients and other construction professionals.

Prospective managers who pursue a postsecondary education typically major in a construction-related field such as construction science, urban planning, architecture, or civil engineering. Depending on the field of study, course work may include classes in project control and development, construction methods, building design, and cost estimating, among other topics. Course work usually includes classroom lectures and hands-on experience.

Construction management majors also study accounting, management, and business law to prepare them for the business side of this career. And since construction managers use construction-specific and financial software often, computer science classes are usually part of this plan of study.

Certification and Licensing

No license or certification is required for this career. However, interested individuals can earn a construction management certificate through the American Institute of Constructors or the Construction Management Association of America. To do so, applicants must pass a written exam and have a required amount of work experience. Certification is prestigious. It indicates that the holder is an expert in construction management, and it may help the holder advance in this career field.

Volunteer Work and Internships

One way individuals can learn more about this career is by working on a construction crew. Contractors often hire high school or college students as laborers during the summer. Being part of a construction project gives individuals a chance to explore the construction field and to observe a construction manager in action.

College students majoring in a construction-related field have the option of doing a summer internship in construction management. Many large construction companies hire paid and unpaid college interns to work alongside construction managers. Interns gain real-world experience in both the construction and business sides of this career. Mentored by seasoned professionals, interns help prepare documents, procure materials, coordinate with subcontractors, and develop project schedules, among other tasks. The experience helps candidates broaden their knowledge and skills and provides them with practical work experience and business contacts that can help them gain full-time employment in the future.

Skills and Personality

Construction managers must be knowledgeable about the different aspects of construction. They should also be strong leaders who possess good interpersonal and communication skills. These supervisors must be able to get along with workers and subcontractors, as well as motivate various team members to do their best work. Settling disputes, offering feedback, leading meetings, and fostering good group dynamics are essential aspects of this skill set. So is being capable of clearly expressing ideas orally and in writing to the many people they interact with on a daily basis. By communicating effectively, construction managers ensure that there is no confusion about what a project entails or what particular roles and responsibilities each team member has.

Other skills that help these experts be strong leaders include being organized and being detail oriented. Construction managers coordinate every aspect of a building project. Managing scheduling, budgets, safety and code issues, and the actual construction process can be overwhelming if these duties are not handled in an orderly, methodical fashion. Small mistakes can lead to costly delays; large mistakes can result in safety issues both for the crew and the structure. But no matter how skilled a construction manager is, problems may arise. These professionals must be good problem solvers who are flexible and able to make changes when necessary.

Moreover, since many construction managers are self-employed, in order to succeed they must be astute businesspeople who understand not only the construction industry but also finance. In bidding on a job, for example, they must take into account the cost of labor and materials, competitors' prices, the client's budget, and current market values. As New York contractor Ruben J. explains in a July

2014 blog post on Contractor Talk: "There are two distinct skill sets involved in running your own business. The first in this field is clearly being very skilled at construction. . . . The second is the skill set used to run, grow, and maintain a business—the same skill set used by any business owner. . . . By remembering that the business portion of contracting and construction is as important as the skills of the crews, I have been able to grow a viable and profitable company."

On the Job

Employers

According to the BLS, about 57 percent of construction managers are self-employed. Others are employed by residential and nonresidential construction companies, civil engineering firms, and real estate developers.

Working Conditions

Construction managers work indoors in an office setting. They also spend a lot of time outdoors at construction sites, which are often noisy, dusty, and dirty. Though their work is not dangerous, they must take safety precautions like wearing a hard hat and work boots since the presence of construction debris, construction vehicles, and machinery can lead to accidents. Moreover, since these experts often manage more than one project at a time, they often travel between construction sites.

Some construction managers have to travel to projects that are located out of their home area. This often involves staying overnight or even longer. In fact, it is not uncommon for managers to be away from home for extended periods while supervising a distant project.

Most construction managers work full time. They may have to work irregular hours and weekends to meet deadlines and in response to building emergencies. This job can be stressful. Meeting budget requirements and deadlines, coping with construction delays caused by unpredictable weather or other factors, and managing crew members are huge tasks that can contribute to a supervisor's stress, especially when things do not go as planned.

Earnings

The BLS reports that as of May 2014, annual wages for construction managers ranged from about $50,990 to $150,250, with a mean salary of about $94,590. Out of one hundred possible different careers in a variety of fields, *U.S. News & World Report* ranks this career as the nineteenth best-paying. Earnings depend on the individual's experience and education, as well as the location of the employer. According to the BLS, the states with the highest mean salary for this job are New Jersey, $131,130; Alaska, $124,550; Rhode Island, $119,330; Pennsylvania, $116,420; and Delaware, $110,540. In addition to a base salary, in some cases these specialists receive bonuses based on the project and whether work is completed on budget and in the scheduled time frame.

Construction managers who are not self-employed usually receive employee benefits such as health insurance, paid sick days and vacation days, retirement benefits, and travel reimbursement. Self-employed individuals do not receive employee benefits.

Opportunities for Advancement

There are many opportunities for individuals to advance in this career field. Those employed by large companies can advance to top-level management positions in which they supervise other construction managers. With experience, construction managers can start their own general contracting construction firm. They can also get into real estate development or larger commercial projects, which are more challenging and more lucrative. In a November 2014 blog post on Contractor Talk, Andrew Gregor, co-owner of CG&H Builders of Celina, Ohio, explains how he advanced in his career: "After high school I went to work full-time at [a local construction company]. . . . I worked at that company for 6 years. . . . I was a crew leader for a few years with that company. It was at that company I met and worked with my current business partner. . . . We decided to go into business for ourselves. . . . We have been involved in a wide range of projects from unique custom homes to working on commercial sites for a graphics company. I can't imagine doing anything else."

What Is the Future Outlook for Construction Managers?

The BLS estimates that employment opportunities for construction managers will grow by 16 percent between 2012 and 2022. This is better than average. Spurring this growth is the need for qualified professionals to supervise projects aimed at improving aging infrastructure throughout the United States. The increased complexity of building projects and the trend toward the construction of environmentally sound "green" construction and electronically controlled "smart" structures, too, should increase the need for experts to manage such projects.

Find Out More

American Council for Construction Education (ACCE)
1717 N. Loop 1604 East, Suite 320
San Antonio, TX 78232-1570
phone: (210) 495-6161
e-mail: acce@acce-hq.org
website: www.acce-hq.org

The ACCE is an organization that promotes, supports, and accredits postsecondary construction education. It provides information about accredited postsecondary construction education programs, posts job openings, and provides links to scholarship opportunities.

American Institute of Constructors (AIC)
PO Box 26334
Alexandria, VA 22314
phone: (703) 683-4999
website: www.professionalconstructor.org

The AIC is a professional organization of construction professionals. It provides information about certification opportunities, industry news, and educational events.

Associated General Contractors of America (AGC of America)
2300 Wilson Blvd., Suite 300
Arlington, VA 22201
phone: (703) 548-3118
e-mail: info@agc.org
website: www.agc.org

AGC of America is an association of general and specialty contractors. In addition to offering industry information, construction data, and education and training programs, it sponsors a number of scholarships, including workforce development scholarships and scholarships for college students.

Construction Management Association of America (CMAA)
7926 Jones Branch Dr., Suite 800
McLean, VA 22102-3303
phone: (703) 356-2622
e-mail: info@cmaanet.org
website: http://cmaanet.org

The CMAA is a professional organization of construction managers. It offers certification, training, and educational opportunities; industry news; job postings; special events; and local chapters throughout the United States.

Electrician

What Does an Electrician Do?

Electricians install, repair, and maintain electrical systems, which provide communities with power for light, heat, air-conditioning, and communication systems, among other uses. These men and women are skilled professionals whose work involves complex tasks. For instance, when working on new construction, electricians typically follow blueprints that show the designated location of circuits, wiring, outlets, and other electrical equipment in the building.

Guided by these specifications, they measure, cut, and install special insulated tubing known as conduit in the structure. Once the conduit is in place, they run electrical wires and cables through it, connecting the wires to the incoming electrical service. They also connect the wires to lighting fixtures, circuit breakers, switches, and outlets, all of which they install. They install venting systems and specialized circuits for heating and cooling systems, too. After completing an installation, they test all the circuits for safety and functionality and make adjustments as needed. This is very important because faulty wiring can cause fires.

At a Glance:
Electrician

Minimum Educational Requirements
High school diploma

Personal Qualities
Mathematical
Detail oriented

Certification and Licensing
State license

Working Conditions
Indoors and outdoors

Salary Range
About $31,170 to $85,590

Number of Jobs
As of 2015 about 566,930

Future Job Outlook
Better than average

In addition to working on new construction, electricians are instrumental in maintaining and repairing existing electrical systems. In this capacity, they test and troubleshoot electrical systems and equipment and repair or replace defective items as needed. Some electricians specialize in this type of work. They are known as maintenance electricians. Those who opt to specialize in new construction are known as construction electricians.

Electricians can further specialize as residential, commercial, or industrial electricians. As the titles imply, residential electricians limit their work to homes, commercial electricians work on commercial structures, and industrial electricians work in large plants where they deliver electrical power to machinery and set up automation systems, among other tasks. Other specialists work as outside electricians or lineworkers. These individuals work on outdoor electrical lines and in power plants.

Many electricians handle multiple specialties. Muncie, Indiana, electrician Vernon Ward, who is profiled in a March 2013 article in the *Muncie Star Press*, is one of these generalists. In his long career he has performed a wide range of electrical jobs. Among other tasks, he has installed backup generators in government buildings, wired new construction, rewired lights in city parks, and wired self-service gas station pumps with devices that shut the pumps off electronically when the prepaid amount is reached.

No matter whether an electrician is a generalist or a specialist, to ensure a building's safety, all electricians must be familiar with and follow state and local building and electrical codes. And they must be adept at using a variety of tools ranging from simple items like pliers and screwdrivers to more complex tools like voltage meters, electric soldering guns, and testing devices like an oscilloscope, a machine that analyzes electrical signals.

How Do You Become an Electrician?

Education

Electricians should have a high school diploma with a strong background in math. Electricians are constantly measuring and then cal-

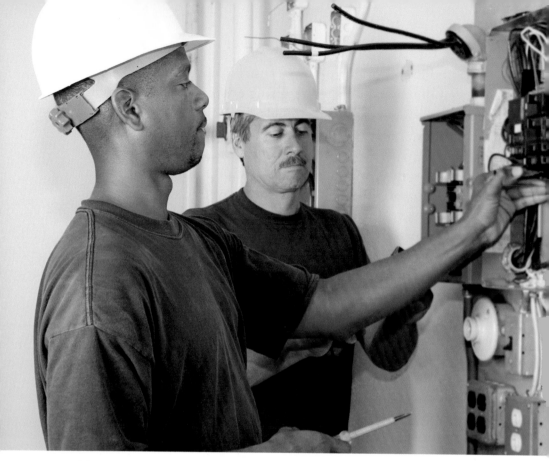

Electricians check a building's wiring and circuits to make sure everything functions properly. The work of an electrician includes installation, repair, and maintenance of electrical systems that provide light, heat, air, and communications.

culating measurements and electrical voltage. They use algebraic formulas and basic arithmetic in making electrical calculations. And they use trigonometry to determine the correct angle for bending conduit and the distance between bending points. Classes in industrial arts, which give students the opportunity to become familiar with different tools, and classes in electronics are also helpful. The latter introduces students to electrical theory.

After graduating from high school, there are a number of ways individuals can become an electrician. Some electricians start out by working as an electrician's helper. These individuals gain knowledge of the profession through informal on-the-job training. Others attend a technical school or adult training center, where they take classes in basic electronics, circuitry, safety, and electrical calculations. In a

March 2013 article in the *Berkshire Eagle*, Jack Blume, a Sheffield, Massachusetts, electrician and instructor at an adult training center that prepares electricians, explains that the class work involves "lots of calculation, a lot of math to it. I tell them, 'This is the stuff you went to sleep on and said I'll never need.' The formulas are algebraic. They spend a lot of time on the formulas."

Another popular way individuals learn this trade is by serving an apprenticeship. An apprenticeship combines classroom instruction in subjects related to this career with on-the-job work experience. Apprentices are closely supervised by experienced electricians known as journeyworkers. Acting as mentors, journeyworkers pass on the skills and knowledge they have developed to apprentice electricians. Apprenticeships are paid positions, and the training is free. To qualify for a program, candidates must be at least eighteen years old, have a high school diploma with one year of algebra, and pass an aptitude test and a substance abuse screening. Some individuals enter an apprenticeship program directly after graduating from high school, whereas others enter a program after working as an electrician's helper and/or attending a technical school.

A number of groups such as the International Brotherhood of Electrical Workers, a labor union, and the Independent Electrical Contractors, an electrical contractor association, sponsor apprentice programs. Electrician apprenticeships usually last four years and require that individuals complete a minimum of 144 hours of technical training and 2,000 hours of on-the-job training each year. Candidates who successfully complete an apprenticeship become journeyworkers. Journeyworkers are considered skilled electricians who can work independently and can hire and train apprentices. After a year as a journeyworker, individuals can become master electricians by completing additional classroom training. Just as the name implies, master electricians are considered masters of the craft and can supervise journeyworkers.

Certification and Licensing

Most states require that electricians be licensed. To become licensed, electricians must successfully complete a written exam. It tests a candidate's knowledge of electrical theory, electrical formulas, state and local building codes, and national electrical codes.

Volunteer Work and Internships

Individuals interested in becoming an electrician can learn more about the profession by working on a construction crew. Doing so gives prospective electricians a chance to observe and interact with professional electricians. Job shadowing an electrician for at least one day is another way to learn about the profession.

Individuals can also learn more about electronics by pursuing hobbies that involve electronics, such as working on electronic hobby kits. Being a member of the lighting crew for a school play or community theater production is another way to learn more about electronics.

Skills and Personality

Working as an electrician is a challenging task that requires a range of skills. These professionals deal with complex issues and make lots of decisions each day. They should be good critical thinkers and problem solvers who are knowledgeable about electronics, electrical theory, and electrical safety. This combination of knowledge and skills helps them diagnose electrical problems and come up with quick, well-thought-out solutions. As master electrician JRaef explains in a November 2014 article on the website Electrician Talk, "Having BEEN 'a 'lectrician,' I know what it's like to be EXPECTED to be able to solve any problem. . . . I think it takes a special breed of person to WANT to do this kind of work."

Electricians should also have good math skills so that they can do electrical calculations. Since many of these calculations involve fractions, they should be adept at working with fractions and with converting between fractions, percentages, and whole numbers. Being tech-savvy is also vital. These professionals are often charged with wiring modern "smart homes," in which lighting, security systems, and electrical appliances can be controlled via smartphone and tablet apps. Doing this type of work requires that individuals understand the technology involved.

In addition, these men and women should be good listeners who are able to take and follow directions well. This is especially important during the apprenticeship stage since an important way apprentices learn their craft is by following the instructions of seasoned professionals. Paying careful attention to detail is another trait that helps people become successful electricians. Electricians must be methodical in their work. Small mistakes can cause injuries or even fatalities to themselves and other workers, as well as put the building and its occupants at risk in the future.

In addition, electricians need a variety of physical abilities. They should have good eye-hand coordination and excellent color vision. The latter is essential since wires are often color coded. Also, they should be manually dexterous and physically fit. Being an electrician involves a number of physically challenging tasks. These professionals often lift and carry heavy equipment, climb ladders, get in and out of tight spaces, and work in awkward positions. Crouching, kneeling, bending, and reaching for long periods are a part of the job. As Hayley, a New Zealand electrician, explains in an interview on the Careers New Zealand website, "You've got to be willing to get pretty dirty in your work. . . . You'll be crawling under houses, and in ceilings, and doing a lot of hard jobs. . . . So you've got to be willing to get a few cuts and scratches here and there."

On the Job

Employers

Most electricians work for electrical or wiring installation contractors. Some work for utility systems, government agencies, and institutions like hospitals or factories that require in-house electricians. According to the BLS, approximately 9 percent of electricians are self-employed.

Working Conditions

Electricians work indoors and outdoors. In the course of their career, they work on a variety of projects at many different locations, which may require them to travel. They often have to work in hot, cramped spaces and may be exposed to dirt, dust, and loud noise. Electricians are subjected to a number of on-the-job hazards and have a higher rate of injury than the national average. Common injuries include electric shock, falls, and burns. They may also suffer from repetitive stress injuries to the knees, back, and hands. Wearing safety equipment and following safety rules, however, help lessen an electrician's chance of accidents and injuries.

Most electricians work a standard forty-hour workweek. They may have to work evenings and weekends. The weather, construction deadlines, and electrical emergencies affect their work schedules. Generally, they are paid for working overtime. Self-employed electricians set their own schedules.

Earnings

An electrician's earnings depend on his or her level of experience and the geographic location of the employer. The BLS reports that as of May 2014, salaries for this profession range from about $31,170 to $85,590, with a mean annual wage of $54,520. Typically, apprentices are paid the least and master electricians the most. Geographically, the BLS reports that mean salaries are highest in the following states: Alaska, $78,800; Illinois, $69,940; New York, $69,820; Oregon, $68,690; and New Jersey, $67,570.

With the exception of self-employed electricians, most electricians receive employee benefits in addition to their salary. These may include health, dental, and life insurance; paid sick leave; paid vacation days; and retirement benefits.

Opportunities for Advancement

Electricians can expect to receive higher wages and more responsibilities as they advance from apprentice status to journeyworker and from journeyworker to master electrician. In addition, since master electricians are permitted to hire and supervise electricians of all levels, they may advance to supervisory positions in which they oversee teams of electricians, or they can establish their own electrical contracting business.

What Is the Future Outlook for Electricians?

The BLS estimates that between 2012 and 2022, employment for electricians will grow by 20 percent, which is much better than average for all occupations. The development and popularity of electrical devices and electrical equipment, and the need to upgrade older wiring systems to accommodate such equipment, should spur this growth.

Find Out More

Electrical Training Alliance
301 Prince George's Blvd., Suite D
Upper Marlboro, MD 20774
e-mail: office@njatc.org
website: www.electricaltrainingalliance.org

The Electrical Training Alliance is a publisher of educational materials for the electronics industry. It provides information about apprenticeships, certifications, and industry news.

International Brotherhood of Electrical Workers (IBEW)
900 Seventh St. NW
Washington, DC 20001
phone: (202) 833-7000
website: www.ibew.org

The IBEW is a labor union that represents electricians. It offers information about the industry, joining the union, and job postings.

International Electrical Contractors (IEC)
4401 Ford Ave., Suite 1100
Alexandria, VA 22302
phone: (703) 549-7351
e-mail: info@ieci.org

The IEC is a trade association of electricians. It provides information about the industry, becoming an electrician, electrical safety, and a magazine about electrical news.

National Electrical Contractors Association
3 Bethesda Metro Center, Suite 1100
Bethesda, MD 20814
phone: (301) 657-3110
website: www.necanet.org

The professional organization of electrical contractors offers information about careers in electrical contracting, licensing requirements, apprenticeships, and job postings.

Landscape Architect

What Does a Landscape Architect Do?

Landscape architects plan and design outdoor spaces for businesses, home owners, and governments. Their work covers a vast range of projects, including parks; institutional, corporate, and academic campuses; and private and public gardens. It can also be seen in planned communities, green roofs, public monuments, and historic and natural preservation and restoration projects. The latter includes the restoration of natural places such as wetlands, mined areas, and forested land that have been disturbed by humans. According to the American Society of Landscape Architects (ASLA), "Landscape architects play an important role in environmental protection by designing and implementing projects that respect both the needs of people and of our environment." For example, in 2015 the ASLA organized the Chinatown Green Street Demonstration Project in Washington, DC. The project involves the creation of interconnected green spaces that beautify the neighborhood, reduce air pollution, and control storm water runoff.

As part of their job, landscape architects take on many different tasks. Before beginning a project, they meet with prospective clients to discuss the client's vision of the project and its scope, funding, and purpose. Next, landscape architects make a careful study of the proposed site. As part of the study, they measure the site, noting the area's elevation, shady and sunny areas, and the soil and drainage conditions. In addition, they identify existing plant and animal life, as well as any existing structures and utilities. They do this so that proposed land features and structures harmonize with what is already there. For projects that involve creation of a new park or restoration of a polluted site into a safe green space, landscape architects often consult with architects, city and zoning officials, civil engineers, urban planners, and others.

With all this knowledge in hand, landscape architects develop a comprehensive multipage plan for the site. They use computer-assisted design software to produce detailed two- and three-dimensional design plans and models. The plans also include information about irrigation and drainage, lighting and water features, seating areas, and hardscape designs such as the location of pavement and stepping stones. A site map, cost estimates and breakdown, a work schedule, and other specifications that are relevant to the project are other parts of the design package.

The plans are presented to the client for feedback. Once the client approves the plans, landscape architects hire a landscape contractor, who is responsible for the actual plantings and other physical labor. While work is being done on the site, landscape architects act as project managers. In this capacity, they supervise and monitor the work. They remain attached to the project until the job is completed and clients give their final approval of the work.

How Do You Become a Landscape Architect?

Education

This career requires that individuals have a minimum of a bachelor's degree from a program accredited through the Landscape Architectural Accreditation Board. High school students interested in becoming a landscape architect should therefore take college preparatory classes. Classes in plant science, art, design, and computer technology, especially those in computer-assisted drafting, provide students with an introduction to some of the skills they need in this career. Also essential are classes in speech and language arts, which help students become better communicators, an ability that landscape architects use in preparing reports and presentations and in communicating with the various individuals involved in a project.

In college, most landscape architects pursue either a bachelor of landscape architecture (BLA) or a bachelor of science in landscape architecture (BSLA) degree. Both cover a range of topics in horticulture, art, natural and social science, and construction technology relevant to this occupation. For instance, classes in horticulture cover topics such as soil analysis, plant growth, and plant preservation. Classes in the fundamentals of landscape architecture and design give students a background in subjects like site analysis, spatial considerations, planting design, and aesthetic principles. Graphic arts classes provide students with instruction and hands-on studio work using landscape design software. Other classes in landscape construction cover topics like construction and landscape materials and machinery, building and paving methods, irrigation techniques, and sustainable development. Students also take related classes in drawing, urban planning, geology, and environmental science, among other topics.

Certification and Licensing

Almost all states require that landscape architects be licensed. Although licensure requirements vary by state, most require that candidates hold at least a bachelor's degree from an accredited landscape architecture program, have one to four years' work experience in the field, and successfully complete the Landscape Architect Registration Exam, a written exam that tests a candidate's knowledge of soil, plants, and environmental laws. Thirty states also require that licensed landscape architects complete continuing education classes in order to maintain their license.

Some landscape architects choose to obtain other voluntary certification, such as that of a certified arborist. Arborists are expert in the cultivation of trees and woody plants. Landscape architects may

A landscape architect considers possible changes to a garden plan. Landscape architects plan and design outdoor spaces. These spaces might be for schools and businesses or for private homes or even for entire planned communities.

also acquire certification as an accredited professional in Leadership in Energy and Environmental Design (LEED) construction, which indicates that he or she is an expert in sustainable "green" construction. Both certificates help professionals advance in their careers. In an interview on the ISEEK Green website, Minnesota landscape architect and ecologist Tory Christensen explains: "I'm a certified arborist through the International Society of Arboriculture. I took that test to add credential to what I do within landscape architecture since I do a lot of work with trees and woodland restoration. And that certification helped make me more marketable to potential employers. My other certification is that I'm an accredited professional in LEED. . . . This certificate is helpful to me because as a landscape architect/ecologist, I do a lot of work alongside engineers and architects. I'm heavily involved in the outside aspects of buildings in terms of how the building is placed in the landscape: its storm water impact . . . as well as the general layout of the site. . . . Landscape architects can have a huge role in the green building process."

Volunteer Work and Internships

One way individuals can learn more about landscape architecture is by volunteering to work on a community project aimed at improving parks, hiking trails, river access, and/or other outdoor spaces. Local, state, and national groups, including the National Park Service, seek volunteers for such projects. For example, New York City's Central Park Conservancy, which is responsible for keeping Central Park beautiful, depends on a large group of volunteers, many of whom are involved with maintaining and enhancing the park's landscape. These individuals work closely with landscaping professionals on both large- and small-scale projects. Such experiences enhance a prospective landscape architect's knowledge of horticulture, environmental issues, and landscape design. Many parks also offer education programs and summer internships for high school students.

Other internship opportunities are available for college students. By doing an internship, young people can learn more about the profession while gaining valuable hands-on work experience. Interns may be involved in all aspects of a project, from project meetings and site visits, to design, budgeting, and presentations. This type of experience allows them to apply their academic studies to the real world and to make valuable industry connections, which can help them gain full-time employment. In fact, it is not uncommon for firms to hire promising interns upon their graduation. Internship positions may be paid or unpaid, depending on the employer. The ASLA lists internship opportunities on its website, which student members can access. Most colleges also help students find appropriate internship positions.

Skills and Personality

Landscape architecture combines art and science. Individuals who are creative and artistic with a strong interest in nature, horticulture, and environmental protection are often drawn to this occupation. They should have both a good sense of design and analytic skills so that their creations are pleasing in appearance as well as functional.

For example, landscape architects involved in the rebuilding of New Orleans after Hurricane Katrina developed streetscapes that include rain gardens (planted depressions that slow the flow of the water and prevent flooding), decorative rain barrels, and subsurface water storage in an effort to create attractive spaces that help minimize flooding.

Landscape architects also use creativity and logic in solving problems. Throughout the course of any project, problems are sure to arise. These professionals must look at problems from many perspectives, including how different solutions impact the client, the work schedule and budget, plant and animal life, the environment, and people. In so doing, they weigh the strengths and weaknesses of different solutions, carefully evaluating each option before implementing a solution that balances the different demands. Flexibility is also essential to handling problems. Weather conditions can delay work on a project. As project managers, landscape architects have to be able to find ways to move scheduled work around in order to meet deadlines.

The ability to communicate effectively is also essential to this career. These men and women confer with clients, contractors, and other construction professionals. They must be able to explain the details of a project in a way that everyone can understand. This may be through discussion, reports, or graphic communication on paper. In his interview on ISEEK Green, Christensen explains: "Sometimes I'll take an aerial photo of a site I'm working on, import it into Illustrator [a drawing software program] in order to create an easy-to-understand map with arrows, symbols, and text explaining the project to stakeholders." Indeed, landscape architects use a variety of software in their work, including design, drafting, mapping, and word processing programs. They must therefore be tech-savvy. And of course they should be extremely knowledgeable about plants.

On the Job

Employers

Landscape architects work for a variety of employers in both the public and private sectors. Public sector employers include local, state, and federal governments. Engineering firms, architectural firms, landscape architecture firms, and general contractors are among private sector employers. According to the BLS, one in five landscape architects is self-employed.

Working Conditions

These professionals work both indoors and outdoors. They spend about half the time in an office environment. Here they work on designs and models, meet with clients and coworkers, and prepare all the paperwork involved in planning a project. They spend the rest of their work time at job sites.

Most landscape architects work a traditional forty-hour workweek. However, when facing a project deadline, they may work longer hours.

Earnings

Earnings for this profession depend on an individual's experience and the location of the employer. The BLS reports that as of 2014, salaries for landscape architects ranged from about $40,690 to $106,120, with a mean salary of $69,530. It further reports that mean salaries are highest in the following states: California, $82,880; Connecticut, $79,520; Massachusetts, $79,450; Maryland, $79,050; and Missouri, $76,900. Most landscape architects also receive employee benefits, which vary by employer but usually include health insurance, retirement benefits, paid vacation time, and sick leave. Those individuals who are self-employed do not receive benefits.

Opportunities for Advancement

Licensed landscape architects with successful work experience can advance to a managerial position, in which they oversee other landscape professionals and often receive a share of the firm's annual profits. They can also strike out on their own and open their own firm.

What Is the Future Outlook for Landscape Architects?

According to the BLS, between 2012 and 2022 employment opportunities for these professionals should grow by 14 percent, which is faster than average for all occupations. Environmental concerns such as pollution, deforestation, and water scarcities should propel the demand for landscape architects to help solve these problems. Urban growth and the increasing demand for green spaces should also create opportunities for these specialists.

Find Out More

American Society of Landscape Architects (ASLA)
636 Eye St. NW
Washington, DC 20001
phone: (202) 898-3736
website: www.asla.org

The ASLA is a professional society of landscape architects, students, and people interested in landscape architecture. It provides lots of information about the career, accredited college programs, scholarships, and license requirements. It sponsors student chapters in colleges throughout the country.

Cultural Landscape Foundation
1711 Connecticut Ave. NW, Suite 200
Washington, DC 20009
phone: (202) 483-0553
website: http://tclf.org

This nonprofit organization helps people learn about the importance of landscape architecture and also sponsors educational events. The foundation's website has profiles of landscape architects as well as publications.

Landscape Architects Network
website: http://landarchs.com

This website is dedicated to promoting landscape architecture. It provides articles, news, pictures of different landscape architecture projects, and profiles of landscape architects, who talk about their work.

Landscape Architecture Foundation
website: https://lafoundation.org

This organization is made up of landscape professionals dedicated to supporting the enhancement and preservation of the environment. It funds student-faculty landscape research projects, offers scholarships to landscape architecture students, and provides interviews with prominent landscape architects.

Plumber

What Does a Plumber Do?

Plumbers install, repair, and maintain pipes and pipe systems. Some of these systems supply gas to ovens; clean water to sinks, showers, and toilets; or heating and cooling to buildings. Other systems carry steam that is used to drive turbines in power plants whereas still others transport waste produced in manufacturing away from factories. Without proper plumbing, buildings would not have running water, flush toilets, or gas for cooking and heating, among other things. The work of plumbers helps keep buildings hygienic and safe and improves the quality of people's lives.

Plumbers are involved in new construction and in servicing existing plumbing. A plumber's involvement in new construction starts before the building process begins. One of the first things plumbers are tasked with is studying blueprints of the proposed structure in order to determine where pipes should be laid and the size and angle of each pipe. Then, before the foundation is poured, plumbers install the building's drainage system, which includes sewage pipes. This system acts as the means by which waste can be transported away from the building. This early work is known as groundwork. Before

At a Glance:
Plumber

Minimum Educational Requirements
High school diploma

Personal Qualities
Mechanical
Good problem solver

Certification and Licensing
State license

Working Conditions
Mainly indoors

Salary Range
About $29,470 to $88,180

Number of Jobs
As of 2015 about 372,570

Future Job Outlook
Better than average

A plumber replaces the pipes on a bathroom sink. Plumbers install, repair, and maintain pipes that supply gas, water, heating, and cooling to homes and businesses. They also install and repair waste and drainage systems.

installing the pipes and pipe fittings for groundwork, and before installing other pipes and fittings, plumbers must measure, cut, and bend the pipes to the required sizes and angles.

Later, when the structure is partly erected, plumbers are charged with a job known as a "rough in." This involves making holes in walls in order to install pipes and pipe fittings to wet areas of the building. Some of these pipes will carry hot and cold water; others will transport waste. As part of this process, plumbers must connect different pipes to each other. They often use welding equipment to do this.

Another task that plumbers do involves installing ventilation pipes through the building's roof. These pipes draw in outside air. The pressure of the air helps push waste downward to drain pipes. Ventilation pipes also expel harmful gases and unpleasant odors from the building.

Finally, when the building is almost finished, plumbers connect the pipes to plumbing fixtures such as bathtubs, toilets, and sinks, and to appliances such as dishwashers and garbage disposals. Plumbers also lay pipes to stoves that connect to gas lines. And they install and repair heating and cooling systems. Some plumbers specialize in this task. They are known as heating and cooling, or HVAC, technicians.

Plumbers also repair and maintain plumbing in existing buildings. In this capacity they travel to homes and commercial buildings where they troubleshoot and then fix or replace burst, clogged, leaky, and broken pipes, drains, faucets, water heaters, and heating and cooling units. In troubleshooting plumbing problems, they use air and water pressure gauges to test pipes for leaks.

Plumbers are also involved in the plumbing of commercial and residential remodeling projects. They work on updating kitchens and bathrooms and on adding wet areas to homes and businesses. In an interview on the website Explore the Trades, New Jersey plumber David Nowicki talks about how much he enjoys this part of his work: "I get a good feeling fixing things and it's a great sense of accomplishment when you can turn an empty room into a full working bathroom, laundry room or kitchen."

How Do You Become a Plumber?

Education

Plumbers should be high school graduates. In preparation for this career, high school students should take classes in math, physics, and industrial arts. Plumbers use much of what they learned in these classes on the job. For instance, being comfortable working with numbers is important in this profession because plumbers have to take measurements, and many of these measurements require that plumbers convert fractions to decimals or vice versa. Plumbers also use basic geometry to figure out the volume of containers like water tanks or the size of three-dimensional objects. They use physics to understand force and how to control it, particularly the force of water under pressure. Industrial arts classes give them experience using different tools.

After high school, to become a licensed plumber, candidates must do an apprenticeship. Apprentice programs are a mix of technical education and paid work experience. Apprenticeships usually last four to five years and include about 246 hours of classroom training annually. These classes focus on practical matters like how to safely use tools and materials and how to read blueprints, as well as introduce students to state plumbing codes.

Apprentices spend about two thousand hours per year on the job. They are trained by journeyman plumbers. Apprentices physically assist their mentors in all aspects of the job. This includes installing gas piping, waste and ventilation systems, and water supply systems, as well as servicing existing plumbing. In a January 2015 interview on the Equal Rights Advocate website, April, an Oregon apprentice plumber, talks about her experience: "I know that each and every day when I wake up, it will never be the same as the day before. I will be learning something different every day, even if it is on the same job site. I will benefit from Journeymen and other apprentices offering advice and helping me by explaining the work and maybe even showing me a faster way to do something."

To qualify to participate in an apprentice program, candidates must be at least eighteen years old, have a high school diploma, and pass an aptitude test and a substance abuse screening. Local chapters of the United Association of Journeymen and Apprentices of the Plumbing and Pipe Fitting Industry of the United States sponsor apprenticeships, as do many plumbing contractors. These programs are free. Trade and vocational schools also offer apprenticeship programs. These, however, charge tuition.

Certification and Licensing

Most states require that plumbers be licensed. Requirements for licensing vary by state. Typically, to obtain a license, plumbers must have two to five years of work experience, and they must pass an exam that tests their knowledge of plumbing and plumbing codes. Individuals who pass the exam become licensed journeymen plumbers. This allows them to work without supervision. With one to five years of work experience as a journeyworker, these professionals can become licensed master plumbers by successfully completing another exam. Master plumbers can supervise journeyworkers and can go into business for themselves as plumbing contractors.

Plumbers can also take additional classes and tests in order to acquire other voluntary certificates, which help them advance in their field. Individuals interested in water conservation and water-efficient technology, for example, can earn certification as a Green Plumber.

Volunteer Work and Internships

A good way to learn what it is like to be a plumber is by participating in a plumbing internship. Many municipal utility districts and plumbing contractors offer such positions to interested individuals. Interns get to watch and assist plumbers as they do their work, gaining hands-on experience in tasks such as assembling and installing pipes and fixing plumbing fixtures. Internships generally take place during the summer and may be paid or unpaid, depending on the position.

Job shadowing a plumber is another way to learn about this career. Working part-time in a plumbing firm is also helpful. Even doing a job such as answering phones in a plumbing company gives individuals an opportunity to learn more about the plumbing business.

Skills and Personality

Plumbing is hands-on, physical labor. Individuals who are mechanical and have good manual dexterity, eye-hand coordination, and vision do well at this job. These characteristics help plumbers manipulate small objects, line up pipes and pipe fittings correctly, and spot leaks and other problems. Being physically fit is also essential. Plumbers must be able to hold their arms and hands steady while supporting tools and pipes for long periods. They often have to work in cramped spaces and in extreme temperatures. Crouching, reaching, climbing ladders, and lifting heavy equipment are parts of a typical workday. They therefore need strength and stamina. And, because working conditions can be messy, they should not be afraid to get dirty.

They also should have good people skills. Particularly in repair work, plumbers visit the homes of many different people. Allowing a stranger into one's home can be intimidating, particularly for single women or older individuals. To ensure that customers feel comfortable, plumbers should be respectful, nonthreatening, and personable. And they should like helping others. In an interview on the *Daily Mail* website, British plumber Jo Lawrence puts it this way: "I love being a plumber, because I enjoy working with people. There's nothing better than resolving someone's problems."

Indeed, being a skilled and creative problem solver is important, too. These men and women are faced with multiple plumbing problems on a daily basis. Some problems may be routine, whereas others may be quite challenging. Plumbers must use logic and good judgment in analyzing plumbing problems and coming up with the best solution. If one solution does not work, their creative problem-solving ability helps them come up with an alternative. And even if a job proves difficult, these individuals must be persistent in seeing it through to a successful conclusion.

On the Job

Employers

Plumbers are employed by general, plumbing, and heating and cooling contractors. They also work for public utility companies and local government. According to the BLS, about 11 percent of all plumbers are self-employed.

Working Conditions

Plumbers work wherever there are pipes or septic systems. Depending on the job, they may have to work outdoors in bad weather. They often work in tight spaces, which can be hard on an individual's back and knees. Falls from ladders and burns from soldering equipment and hot pipes are other risk factors for this job. In addition, the work can be messy and smelly.

Most plumbers work forty hours per week. Because plumbing emergencies can occur at any time, they may have to work nights and weekends. In most cases plumbers are paid extra for overtime work. Some plumbers travel to a variety of work sites every day.

Earnings

The BLS reports that as of May 2014, annual wages for plumbers range from about $29,470 to $88,180, with a mean annual wage of $54,620. Wages depend on an individual's experience and the location of the employer. Generally, apprentices earn the least. Their starting salary is about half of that earned by a journeyworker. However, they are usually given a raise every six months. The states with the highest mean annual salary for this profession, according to the BLS, are Oregon, $72,440; Illinois, $71,810; Massachusetts, $71,270; New York, $71,120; and Alaska, $70,480. In addition to a base salary, most plumbers also receive employee benefits that include health insurance, paid sick and vacation days, and a retirement plan. Self-employed plumbers do not receive benefits.

Opportunities for Advancement

As plumbers advance from apprentice to journeyworker and from journeyworker to master plumber, they are given more responsibility and compensation. Master plumbers working for plumbing contractors can move into management positions in which they oversee other plumbers. Many master plumbers go into business for themselves.

What Is the Future Outlook for Plumbers?

According to the BLS, employment opportunities for plumbers are expected to grow by 21 percent between 2012 and 2022. This is much better than average. Stricter regulations aimed at saving water are expected to increase the need for plumbers. More and more individuals will be seeking the services of plumbers as they switch from high-water-use plumbing fixtures to more efficient devices such as low-flow toilets and showerheads.

Find Out More

Become a Plumber
website: http://becomeaplumber.weebly.com/index.html

This Canadian website is dedicated to promoting plumbing careers. It provides all kinds of information about the occupation, including videos.

Explore the Trades: Explore Plumbing
phone: (651) 789-3366
website: www.explorethetrades.org/plumbing

This website provides information about plumbing, heating and cooling, and electrical careers, including information on what a plumber does, how to become one, apprenticeships, trade schools, and scholarships.

Plumbing-Heating-Cooling Contractors Association (PHCC)
180 S. Washington St.
PO Box 6808
Falls Church, VA 22046
phone: (800) 533-7694
e-mail: naphcc@naphcc.org
website: www.phccweb.org

The PHCC is a national organization with state and local chapters that represents plumbing and heating and cooling professionals. It offers apprenticeship programs and scholarships. The student section of the website provides information about plumbing and heating and cooling careers.

United Association of Journeymen and Apprentices of the Plumbing and Pipe Fitting Industry of the United States (UA)
901 Massachusetts Ave. NW
Washington, DC 20001
phone: (202) 628-5823
website: www.ua.org

The UA is a labor union representing plumbers and pipe fitters throughout North America. It provides five-year apprenticeship programs for plumber candidates, as well as training for professional plumbers and licensing and certification information.

Surveyor

What Does a Surveyor Do?

Surveyors measure and map the earth. They do this to determine legal property boundaries and to support a wide range of construction projects. Using high-tech equipment, they take precise measurements of the distances and angles between set points in order to gather information that they use to prepare detailed reports, maps, and charts of the area measured.

In any given day, these professionals may be found surveying residential lots, city streets, deepwater areas, and forests, among other sites. As Australian surveyor Daniel Kruimel explains on the surveying website A Life Without Limits, "One day I could be working in a new subdivision making new homes possible for families, the next day in the office experimenting with cutting edge new technology and the day after that out on a boat surveying the ocean floor!"

Through their work, surveyors provide data about the shape, contour, and elevation of the earth's surface, which is used by architects, civil engineers, and other construction professionals for urban development, the construction of new buildings, and large infrastructure projects. Surveying measurements

At a Glance:

Surveyor

Minimum Educational Requirements
Bachelor's degree

Personal Qualities
Mathematical
Strong technical skills

Certification and Licensing
State license required

Working Conditions
Indoors and outdoors

Salary Range
About $32,740 to $93,370

Number of Jobs
As of 2015 about 42,400

Future Job Outlook
About average

are used to establish the exact placement of a new road, a bridge, or a tunnel, as well as to determine where a fence should be located between neighboring yards.

Surveyors also work in fields other than construction, but in construction they have a whole range of tasks. For instance, in an effort to help determine boundary lines, before going out in the field, surveyors research property and survey records of the project site. In the field, surveyors use a variety of electronic equipment to take measurements and record field notes. They also use the Global Positioning System (GPS) to accurately locate specific points. They take their findings back to the office, where they use geographic information system software to create maps, charts, and reports that they present to their clients.

While many surveyors take on a variety of projects, some surveyors specialize in a particular type of surveying. Land surveyors, for example, specialize in surveying tracts of land to determine property boundary lines. Highway or engineering surveyors are involved in surveying land for highway and other infrastructure projects. Other specialists known as geodetic surveyors take measurements of large areas of land, water, and space. Among other things, their work establishes the location of specific points related to construction projects. Hydrographic surveyors are involved in measuring and mapping all types of waterways, which surveying is used in the planning and construction of projects like dams, marinas, and bridges, and in making nautical maps.

Mine surveyors are another group. They survey and make maps of areas aboveground and underground that are used in the design of mines. Other surveyors are involved with oil and gas production. These professionals survey areas in which pipelines will be built.

How Do You Become a Surveyor?

Education

Surveyors are required to have a bachelor's degree. To prepare for this career, high school students should take college preparatory classes. Classes in physics, mathematics, geometry, and trigonometry are especially important since surveyors measure distance, direction, and angles and use computations to help identify survey points. Geography, earth science, and computer science classes, too, are essential. Geography classes help surveyors in mapmaking, and knowledge of geology is required for mine and geodetic surveying. Computer science classes help prepare individuals to work with the computer technology essential to surveying.

In college, prospective surveyors typically major in surveying, civil engineering, or geomatics. The last is a relatively new field that focuses on the use of computer programs designed to analyze and organize geographic data for practical use. Although the course work for each major varies, required classes are likely to include calculus, geometry, geology, geophysics, and geography. Students also take classes specific to surveying. These may cover subjects such as surveying fundamentals, geographic information systems, and digital imaging and mapping, among others. In most cases classroom lectures are accompanied by hands-on practice in computer labs equipped with surveying and mapping technology, as well as outdoor fieldwork.

Certification and Licensing

Surveyors are required to be licensed. Requirements vary by state. Most states require that candidates have a bachelor's degree from a program accredited by ABET, have at least two years of work experience under the supervision of a licensed surveyor, and successfully complete two rigorous written exams. In some cases individuals with an associate's degree may become licensed; however, these individuals need to have significantly more work experience before qualifying to take the licensing exams.

Volunteer Work and Internships

There are many ways individuals can explore this profession. For example, young men can learn quite a bit about surveying by participating in the Boy Scouts Surveying Merit Badge Program. While earning this merit badge, scouts are given the opportunity to use various survey measuring tools, computer equipment, and software, as well as create a survey map. Another way both scouts and nonscouts can learn more about surveying is by volunteering at agencies like the Bureau of Land Management or the US Geological Survey. The latter also offers temporary, flexible schedules and summer employment opportunities for high school and college students age sixteen or older.

By participating in a cooperative education or work-study program, college students can learn more about this occupation. Such programs are organized through colleges. Generally, participants alternate a semester of school with a semester of work. Participants are paid, and they get practical experience in surveying and mapping. This experience can help individuals get a job as a survey intern upon graduation.

Before becoming a licensed surveyor, graduates of an accredited program must work for at least two years as a survey intern under the supervision of a licensed surveyor. Such positions are full-time paid positions that prepare candidates for licensure. The type of work interns do depends on their employer and surveying specialty.

Skills and Personality

In the course of their work, surveyors perform numerous mathematical calculations. They should therefore be skilled in and enjoy using arithmetic, geometry, and trigonometry. An interest in geography, earth science, and technology are other qualities that surveyors need. These men and women work with a wide range of computer hardware and software and other high-tech equipment. Those who keep up with technology and are comfortable using it are best suited to this career.

Another personal quality that is important to this career is being detail oriented. To establish correct boundaries, the measurements and calculations that surveyors take must be precise. Accuracy is also essential in recording the results of a survey in the form of maps, charts, and reports. Being detail oriented also helps surveyors in their search for legal and survey records and land titles.

Moreover, since surveyors are charged with a range of tasks, they should prefer variety in their work, including the mixture of working indoors and outdoors. As surveyor Jon Payne explains on the SurveyorConnect.com website: "We get to work with some pretty high tech tools, do some very interesting problem solving, put some challenging land puzzles together, get outdoors for some fresh air and exercise, spend time inside analyzing data and working our brain and produce a piece of artwork [a survey map] as a deliverable. What's not to like about that!"

In addition to these traits, surveyors should be physically fit. These professionals often walk far distances carrying backpacks and equipment over rough terrain, and they stand for long periods. To do their job, they must be strong and have good stamina, balance, and coordination. Having good vision is essential, too. And since surveyors work with clients, other construction professionals, and survey technicians and interns, they should be able to get along well with others and work both independently and as a team.

On the Job

Employers

According to the BLS, 69 percent of surveyors work for engineering, architectural, and surveying firms. Surveyors also work for local, state, and federal government agencies. Other employers include construction firms, public utilities, firms that supply support activities for water transportation, and mining, oil, and gas extraction companies. Some surveyors are self-employed.

Working Conditions

Surveyors work a traditional forty-hour workweek. They work both indoors in an office and outdoors in the field. Their outdoor work location changes with different projects. Some projects may be in remote areas, which may require a surveyor to be away from home for an extended period. While out in the field, they may be exposed to extreme weather conditions and encounter a variety of wildlife. In a January 2013 article on SurveyorConnect.com, Harold, a Mississippi surveyor, described some of his experiences in the field: "I like the outdoors, except for the times of the year where we have extreme summertime hundred-degree heat and the days of rain in the winter. Two deer walked by my GPS station the other day. I came face-to-face with a garter snake about nose high on a tree limb one time. I have been up over my hip boots in sandy mud in 22 degree weather and wondered if I was going to have to spend the night. I have been startled by a covey of quail, a bedded deer, and turkey getting up literally under my feet. I had to duck one time when a red-tail hawk carrying a squirrel zoomed through where my head was."

Earnings

A surveyor's wages depends on the type of employer, the geographic location of the employer, and individual's level of experience, with survey interns earning less than licensed surveyors. According to the BLS, as of May 2014, annual salaries for this profession ranged from about $32,740 to $93,370, with a mean salary of $60,310. It reports that mean salaries are most lucrative in the following states: California, $81,290; Alaska, $78,290; Rhode Island, $71,160; and Washington, $70,960. Most surveyors receive employee benefits that include health insurance, paid sick and vacation time, and retirement benefits. Self-employed surveyors, however, do not receive such benefits.

Opportunities for Advancement

Surveyors start their careers as interns; once they become licensed they are given more responsibility and increased wages. Experienced licensed surveyors often advance to the position of team leader. In this role they supervise survey interns, surveyor technicians, and other less-seasoned surveyors.

What Is the Future Outlook for Surveyors?

The BLS predicts that between 2012 and 2022, job growth for surveyors will increase by about 10 percent, which is as fast as average for all occupations. Demand is likely to be highest in states rich in gas and oil that require the work of surveyors to help establish drilling sites. In addition to job growth, because many surveyors are reaching retirement age, replacements will be needed to fill these positions. Plentiful opportunities also exist for surveyors willing to relocate to Australia, where there is currently a shortage of these professionals.

Find Out More

Be a Surveyor
331 S. White St.
PO Box 2101
Wake Forest, NC 27588
phone: (919) 556-9848
website: www.beasurveyor.com

This website is sponsored by the North Carolina Society of Surveyors Education Foundation. It provides a variety of information about becoming a surveyor, including information about education, scholarships, and licensing.

National Society of Professional Surveyors (NSPS)
5119 Pegasus Ct., Suite Q
Frederick, MD 21704
phone: (240) 439-4615
website: www.nsps.us.com

The NSPS is a professional society of surveyors. It provides information about what surveyors do, colleges and universities offering surveying programs, licensing, and employment opportunities.

US Geological Survey (USGS)
12201 Sunrise Valley Dr.
Mail Stop 205P
Reston, VA 20192
phone: (888) 275-8745
website: www.usgs.gov

The website of the USGS provides information such as videos about volunteer and job opportunities with the US government for students interested in a career in surveying.

Western Federation of Professional Surveyors (WFPS)
526 S. E St.
Santa Rosa, CA 95404
phone: (707) 578-1130
e-mail: admin@wfps.org
website: www.wfps.org

The WFPS is a regional organization composed of land surveyor organizations representing thirteen western states. It provides information about a career in land surveying, scholarships, and links to state organizations.

Interview with a Construction Manager

Al Sheen is the owner of and construction manager at J.E. Activities, a construction company in New York City. He has worked as a construction manager for thirty years. He specializes in the public sector, affordable housing, and environmental issues. He answered questions about his career by telephone.

Q: Why did you become a construction manager?

A: I don't really know. I, kind of, fell into it. I got a master's degree in urban planning, and when I graduated I worked for the government in New Jersey in the housing sector. Then, I got a job with a general contracting firm. I trained by starting out as a field foreman. Then, I brought in a contract for the firm to manage construction projects for the city of New York. I was named construction manager for those projects, and I liked it. I enjoyed pulling the various parts of a job together. So, I stayed with it and eventually I became the owner of the company.

Q: Can you describe a typical workday?

A: In the morning, I'm touring job sites, troubleshooting. That means I'm coordinating the various trades and the trouble that comes up. For instance, the plumber didn't show up as scheduled or the electrician didn't do the job he was supposed to do, or the architect or engineer's plans are not correct. And, each one impacts the other. I make notes of all the problems; then in the afternoon I go back to the office and follow up with the problems I saw in the field. I make phone calls, do invoices, and create change orders for work that I saw in the field that needs to be done but that wasn't in the original plans. Doing change orders is not as easy as it sounds. Everything has to be done on special forms. All the paperwork has to coordinate with the AIA [American Institute of Architecture] forms. There are hundreds of different boxes on a form. Every line item is listed—framing, floor tiles, wall tiles, roofing, wainscoting, etc., every little aspect of construction has its own box. On a million-dollar project or a gut rehab there can be one hundred line items, and each line item has about six sub-items, which breaks up the scope of a project. So it's complicated. I also go to the bank, make deposits, work on the payroll, write checks to pay subcontractors and suppliers, and I do job costing. That means I figure out how the job is working out financially. This is the only way to see how much income came in versus how much you paid in labor, supplies, permits, and insurance. If the job is losing money, I figure out why, and what I can do to correct it.

Another thing I do happens a few times a year at the start of a new project. I may hold bids, where subcontractors who want to be hired for a particular job turn in bids. I examine all the bids, and compare them. I have to make sure that the bids and the subcontractors are legitimate. I check references, whether the subcontractors are bonded, whether they can produce a letter of credit, and whether their pricing is appropriate. To make this determination, I figure out what each part of the project should cost. If a subcontractor's bid is too high or low, I know there's something wrong. Then I assign jobs based on what I've learned.

Q: What do you like most and least about your job?

A: Most, the satisfaction of putting hundreds of different pieces together like a big jigsaw puzzle and in the end get a finished product. Least, squabbling with subcontractors who want more money than what was agreed upon.

Q: What personal qualities do you find valuable for this type of work?

A: Perseverance and the tenacity to not give up when there are lots of obstacles.

Q: What advice do you have for students who might be interested in this career?

A: Get as many licenses and certifications as possible. They help get you jobs and make you stand out from your peers. I have a state environmental inspector license, city asbestos investigator license, city safety manager certificate, certificates of fitness to use different equipment and machinery. Also, take courses in reading blueprints, lots of places offer it.

Q: What is one thing people may not know about a career as a construction manager?

A: It's more complicated than it sounds because you have to balance different people and issues. Everyone has his own agenda, and your agenda is to get the job done on time, and on or below budget. Yours is the largest agenda, and encompasses everything else.

Other Careers in Architecture and Construction

Bricklayer
Carpet Installer
Civil Engineering Technician
Computer-Assisted Drafting
  (CAD) Technician
Construction and Building
  Inspector
Construction Laborer
Contractor
Cost Estimator
Drywall Installer
Environmental Engineer
Glazier
Heating and Cooling Technician
Heavy Equipment Operator
Historic Preservationist
Interior Decorator

Interior Designer
Ironworker
Landscape Designer
Painter
Paper Hanger
Photogrammetrist
Pipe Fitter
Rigger
Roofer
Solar Photovoltaic Installer
Steamfitter
Stonemason
Structural Steel Detailer
Surveying Technician
Tile and Marble Setter
Urban Planner
Welder

Editor's note: The online *Occupational Outlook Handbook* of the US Department of Labor's Bureau of Labor Statistics is an excellent source of information on jobs in hundreds of career fields, including many of those listed here. The *Occupational Outlook Handbook* may be accessed online at www.bls.gov/ooh.

Index

Picture Credits

About the Author

Barbara Sheen is the author of ninety books for young people. She lives in New Mexico with her family. In her spare time she likes to swim, walk, garden, and cook.